AF604610

WOMEN
IN
GREAT
AUSSIE
SPORTS
RUGBY
LEAGUE
TONY LA TORRACA
REDBACK
publishing

First Published 2023 by
Redback Publishing
PO Box 357 Frenchs Forest NSW 2086
Australia

www.redbackpublishing.com.au
orders@redbackpublishing.com.au

978-1-76140-027-8 HBK

Author: Tony La Torraca
Editor: Caroline Thomas
Designer: Redback Publishing

Original illustrations © Redback Publishing 2023
Originated by Redback Publishing

Acknowledgements
Abbreviations: l—left, r—right, b—bottom, t—top, c—centre, m—middle
We would like to thank the following for permission to reproduce photographs: NRL Imagery Official Photos of National Rugby League, images © shutterstock, images@ Alamy Stock Photo

COVER Ali Brigginshaw by PA Images / Alamy Stock Photo, p4 Grant Trouville / NRL IMAGERY, p5 KIWI FERNS v AUSTRALIAN JILLAROOS 2014 (15752976715).jpg by Naparazzi via Wikimedia Commons, p6 KIWI_FERNS_v_AUSTRALIAN_JILLAROOS_2014_(15755222702).jpg by Naparazzi, via Wikimedia Commons, p7 2880px-Dragons_NRL_Women's_Premiership_players.jpg by MasterMind5991 via Wikimedia Commons, p8t Scott Davis / NRL IMAGERY, p9t Anurat Imaree/Shutterstock, p9b Kezie Apps.jpg by MasterMind5991, via Wikimedia Commons, p10 Jillaroos with 2021 WRLWC.jpg by Fleets via Wikimedia Commons, p11 State of Origin 2 (24 June 2009, Sydney).jpg by Pierre Roudiervia Wikimedia Commons, p12t Shannonevans.jpg by Naparazzi, via Wikimedia Commons, p13 Zain Mohammed / NRL IMAGERY, p14 Nathan Hopkins / NRL IMAGERY, p15b Grant Trouville / NRL IMAGERY, p 15t Gregg Porteous / NRL IMAGERY, P16t Super League XVI match ball.jpg by https://picasaweb.google.com/barrau.gerard dragonsWiganMontpellier2011#5614822316880289810 via Wikimedia Commons, P16b Oliviahiggins.jpg by Naparazzi via Wikimedia Commons, p17 Anthony Kourembanas / NRL IMAGERY, p17b Olivia Higgins.jpg by Naparazzi via Wikimedia Commons, 21t imonekarpani.jpg by Naparazzi via Flickr, p18b NRL Rugby League field.svg by Fred the Oyster via Wikimedia Commons, p21t Simonekarpani.jpg by Naparazzi via Wikimedia Commons, p21b State U18 indoor girls play beach hockey_ (207).jpg by Chris Bartle via Flickr, p22 Grant Trouville / NRL IMAGERY, p23t Maddie Studdon.jpg by Naparazzi via Flickr, p24t Gregg Porteous / NRL IMAGERY, p24b Scott Davis / NRL IMAGERY, p25t KARINA BROWN.jpg by Naparazzi via Flickr, p26t Nellie Doherty, How a courageous duo helped women's rugby league kick off in 1921, image [Public Domain], article by Andrew Ferguson, Sun 23 Dec 2018, 02:01 PM, , 2020 National Rugby League, viewed https://www.nrl.com/news/2018/12/23/how-a-courageous-duo-helped-womens-rugby-league-kick-off-in-1921/, p26b Adelaide, Australia - July 24, 2020.jpg by Nick Brundle Photography, p28t KIWI FERNS v AUSTRALIAN JILLAROOS 2014.jpg by Naparazzi via Flickr, p28b KASEY BADGER.jpg by Naparazzi via Flickr, p29t Jillaroos lift 2021 WRLWC.jpg by Fleets via Wikimedia Commons, p29b ISABELLE KELLY by Naparazzi via Flickr, p30t Grant Trouville / NRL IMAGERY, p30b Scott Davis / NRL IMAGERY

A catalogue record for this book is available from the National Library of Australia

CONTENTS

History 4
Establishment 6
NRL Women's Competition 8
Champions 10
Exciting Skills 12
The Aim of the Game 14
The Rules 16
Player Positions NRLW 18
Training 20
NRLW Teams 2022 22
Awards 24
State of Origin 26
The World Cup 28
Indigenous and Māori All Stars 30
Glossary and Index 32

HISTORY

Women's rugby league is a growing sport in Australia, with a high level of participation at both recreational and professional levels. Women's participation of rugby league has been recorded since the early 1920s and it is now one of Australia's most popular women's team sports.

ARLC

The Australian Rugby League Commission (ARLC) is the national governing body that organises the Australian Women's Rugby League, the Australian women's national team and the nine state governing bodies of the game.

Jessica Sergis

Jess Sergis is one of the biggest stars in the women's game, and a move to the Sydney Roosters has her in prime position to lead a new era of NRLW.

In 2018, she played centre for the St. George Illawarra Dragons in the Women's rugby league Premiership. She represented New South Wales in the 2019 Women's State of Origin match, scoring one try to help the Blues win a fourth-consecutive victory over Queensland. With three tries, a try assist, 21 tackle breaks and an average of 153 metres per match over three appearances in the NRLW regular season, Sergis was named the Dally M NRLW Player of the Year for 2019. She was also named the first-ever RLPA NRLW Player of the Year.

History of Women's Rugby League

In 1976, A women's team was formed in Goulburn to play against the touring New Zealand Manurewa team. They played two matches, one in Goulburn and another at Endeavour Field in Cronulla. By the 1990s, Women's Rugby League competitions were being run in Sydney, the Illawarra and the Australian Capital Territory.

In 1995, Australia hosted a tour by the New Zealand national team. This was the inaugural series of Test Matches for both countries in the Women's Rugby League. Tour matches were played in Sydney, Canberra and Brisbane.

Great Britain's Tour

In 1996, Australia hosted a test match series, with a three-Test tour by the Great Britain women's national rugby league team. Australia claimed their inaugural international win in the First Test in Canberra. Great Britain, however, won the Second Test in Brisbane and the Third Test at Redfern Oval in Sydney to claim a series victory.

Women's Game in Queensland

In Queensland, the women's game began in Brisbane and Ipswich. It expanded in 1998 when a competition commenced in Mackay. By the late 1990s, a National Championship was able to be held. Illawarra beat Brisbane in the 1997 championship final and in 1998, the tournament was held at Pizzey Park in Burleigh Heads. The tournament included teams from Sydney, Canberra, Illawarra, Brisbane, Ipswich and, for the first time, Western Australia. The 1999 tournament was reconfigured to have four state or territory teams. New South Wales beat Queensland in the final, ahead of Western Australia and the Australian Capital Territory.

ESTABLISHMENT

In 2017, the Jillaroos defeated the New Zealand Ferns by 23-16 in the final of the Women's Rugby League World Cup. This was the tipping point that saw the NRL finally announce an inaugural Women's NRL season. The games were proposed in a round-robin format and were scheduled for August 2018, towards the back end of the men's season. A stand-alone State of Origin was also announced.

All Stars

The 2011 men's All Stars match included the first Women's All Stars exhibition match between the Indigenous All Stars and the Women's All Stars. The Women's All Stars won 20-6.

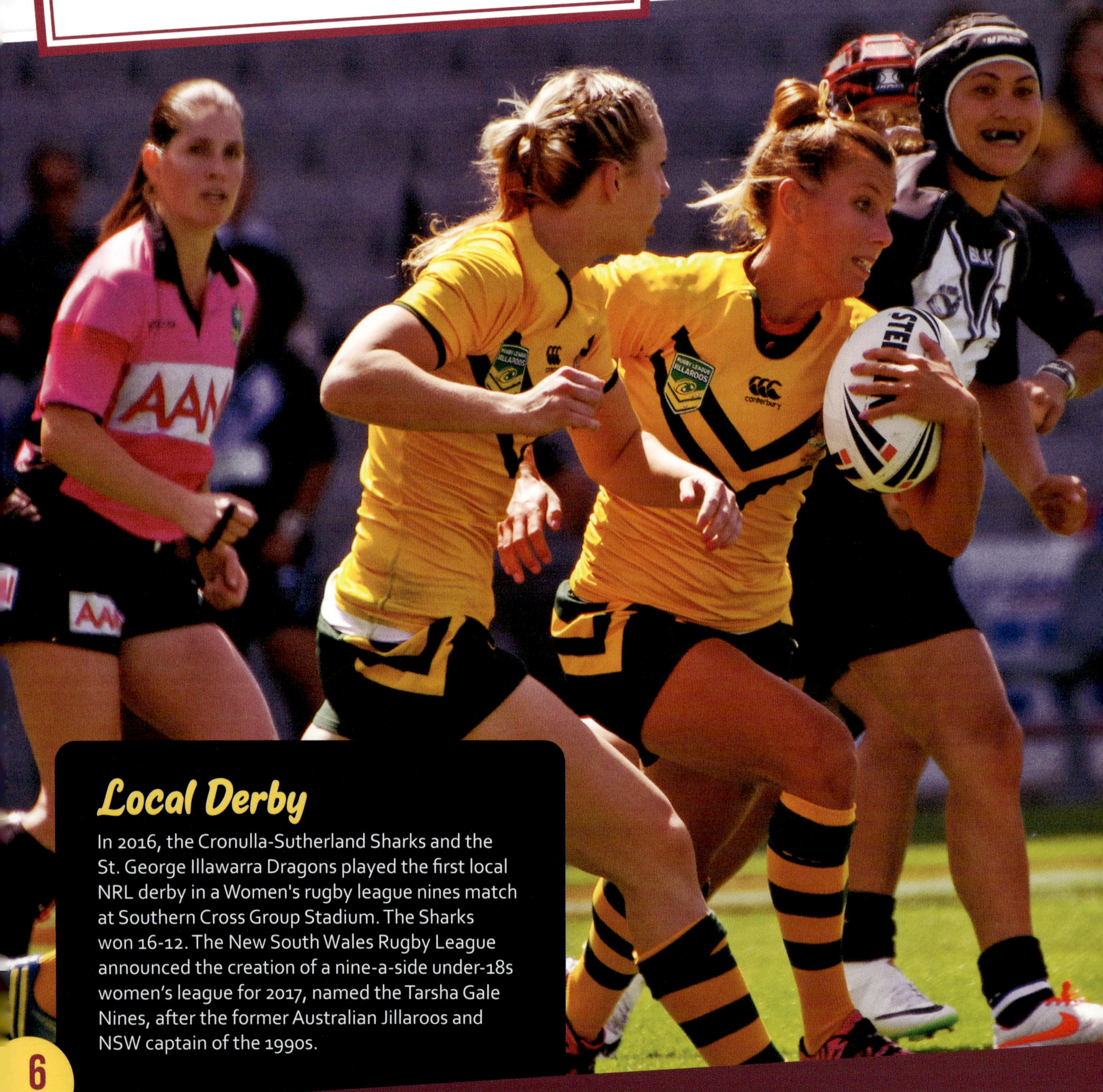

Local Derby

In 2016, the Cronulla-Sutherland Sharks and the St. George Illawarra Dragons played the first local NRL derby in a Women's rugby league nines match at Southern Cross Group Stadium. The Sharks won 16-12. The New South Wales Rugby League announced the creation of a nine-a-side under-18s women's league for 2017, named the Tarsha Gale Nines, after the former Australian Jillaroos and NSW captain of the 1990s.

The St. George Illawarra Dragons were the runners up in 2022

Applying for a Licence

The Newcastle Knights, St. George Illawarra Dragons, Brisbane Broncos, New Zealand Warriors, Sydney Roosters, South Sydney Rabbitohs and Cronulla-Sutherland Sharks all declared their interest in applying for a licence to participate in the inaugural NRL Women's competition. On 27 March 2018, the NRL announced that the Brisbane Broncos, New Zealand Warriors, the St. George Illawarra Dragons and Sydney Roosters had won bids to participate in the inaugural NRL Women's competition, which eventually commenced in September 2018.

2021 Expansion

The Gold Coast Titans, Newcastle Knights and Parramatta Eels joined the competition for the 2021 season, while the Warriors withdrew from the competition.

2023 Expansion

2023 will see the 6th season of the Women's NRL expand to include a further four teams. The Canberra Raiders, the Cronulla Sutherland Sharks, the North Queensland Cowboys and the Wests Tigers will join the competition to play a season of nine rounds followed by semi-finals and a Grand Final.

NRL WOMEN'S COMPETITION

The NRL Women's competition operates on a single-table system, with no divisions, conferences or promotion and relegation from other leagues.

Ali Brigginshaw

Ali Brigginshaw plays for the Brisbane Broncos in the NRL Women's Premiership, primarily a halfback but also playing as a lock, she is the captain of the Broncos, the Jillaroos and Queensland. She captained the Broncos in three Grand Final wins and won the Dally M Medal for female Player of the Year in 2019.

Playing Lists

The competition involves six teams based across two states of Australia, with club playing lists created from scratch in 2018. All players from the 2018 season had to be over the age of 17 and clubs began by nominating a list of their best players to the NRL. Two players from these lists were chosen as marquee players for each club. Clubs could then sign a number of players who had existing connections to their club.

Grand Finals are often played at Stadium Australia at Sydney Olympic Park

Premiership Season

The season operates using a round-robin format, with the top two finishing teams to contest the Grand Final which is to be held on the same day as the men's NRL Grand Final.

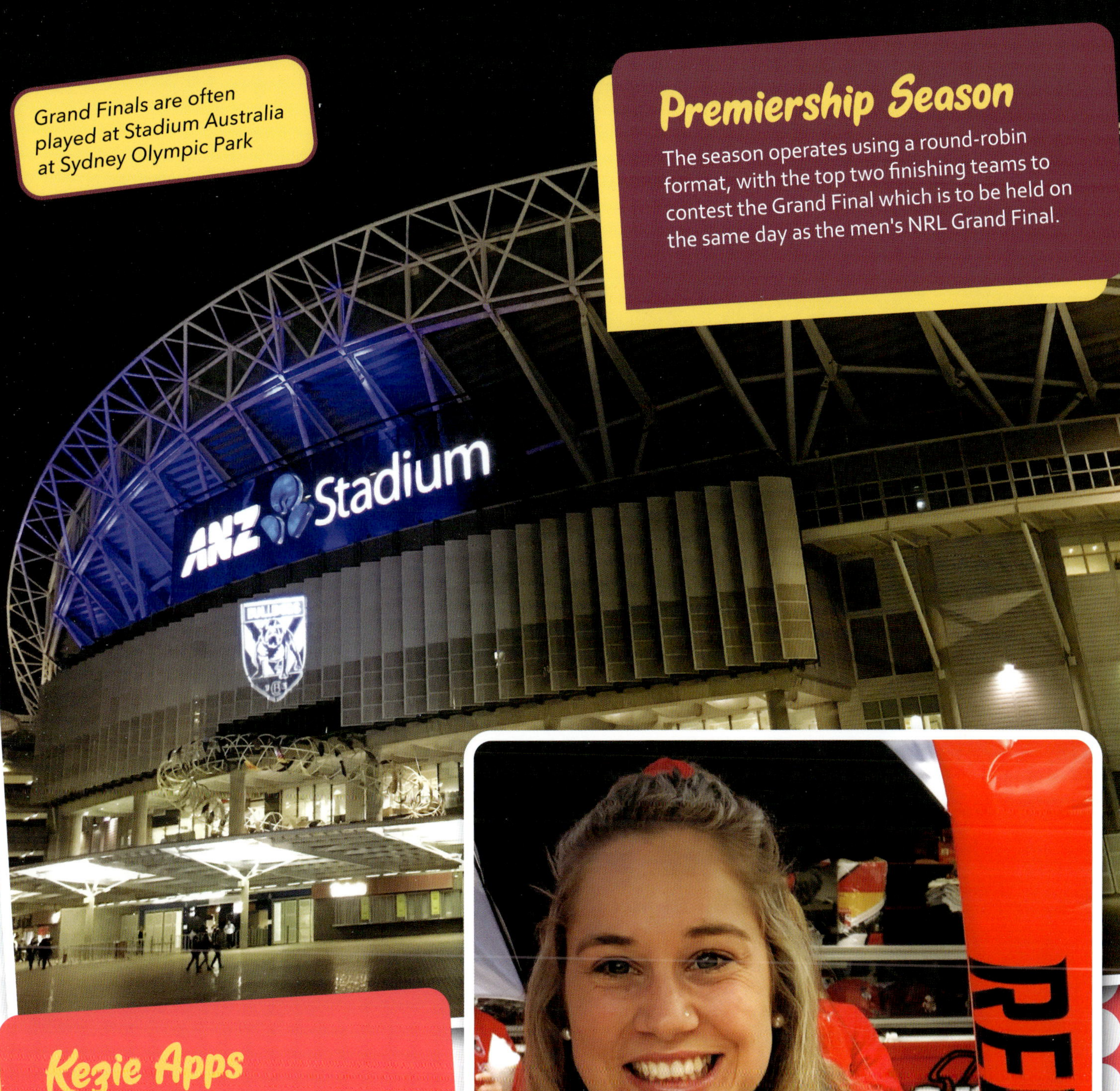

Kezie Apps

The St George Illawarra Dragons joined the NFLW in the inaugural competition held in 2018. Kezie Apps plays as a second-row for the St George Illawarra Dragons in the NRL Women's Premiership and the Wests Tigers in the NSWRL Women's Premiership. She is a mentor for the NSW Women's Country team, is the NSW State of Origin captain and was the Australian Jillaroos co-captain for the World Cup in 2022.

CHAMPIONS

The Australian Jillaroos are current world champions, having won the last three Women's Rugby League World Cup tournaments, in 2013, 2017 and 2022.

Jillaroos

The Jillaroos squad is selected by a panel of national selectors. There are specific tournaments and matches that act as selection trials, including the State of Origin.

Women's Rugby League World Cup

Year	Host	Winner	Winning Score	Runners-up	Runners-up Score
2000	England	New Zealand	26	Great Britain	4
2003	New Zealand	New Zealand	58	NZ Māori	0
2008	Australia	New Zealand	34	Australia	0
2013	England	Australia	22	New Zealand	12
2017	Australia	Australia	23	New Zealand	16
2022	England	Australia	54	New Zealand	4
2025	France	Future Event	–	Future Event	–

State of Origin

The 2020 game was originally due to be played in June at Sunshine Coast Stadium, but was moved to the post-season due to the COVID-19 pandemic. The game was eventually played in Queensland under the State of Origin banner for the first time. Queensland defeated New South Wales 24–18.

The 2021 match is historically notable for being the first Women's State of Origin fixture where the players, coaches and on-field officials were all women.

Selection Rules

Prior to 2019, the Queensland and New South Wales teams were largely selected under residency rules, meaning a number of players represented both states.
In 2019, the eligibility rules were revised to be more in line with the men's State of Origin rules and the residency rule was removed.

State of Origin games draw huge crowds

Who Do You Support?

The NSW Blues

The QLD Maroones

EXCITING SKILLS

NRLW is a fast and exciting game which lasts for 35 minutes each half.

Brain Skills

Rugby league is as much about thinking as it is about physical strength and fitness. During the course of a match, a player will be required to make many quick decisions in regard to passing, evading and setting up play to gain the best possible result.

Kicking

Kicking skills are very important to gain ground and give your team the best field position to score a try. As well as set-piece kicks for goal, players must be able to master dropped kicks and kicks for the touchline, which often require pinpoint accuracy.

Footwork

Evasion is one of the most important rugby league skills. Avoiding or overcoming a tackle gains a team vital metres towards the goal line. Evasion depends on footwork as sheer speed will not always get a player out of trouble. A successful player can change direction while running, swerve, and change pace to deceive opponents.

Ball Handling

Keeping the ball in your team's possession is crucial in rugby league. The key to maintaining possession is good ball handling. A player must know how to receive a pass expertly, and how to pass the ball in a variety of ways.

Destiny Brill

Destiny Brill made her NRLW debut with the Titans in 2022 and represents Queensland in the State of Origin, scoring the Maroons' first try in the 2022 tournament. Brill plays for the Sydney Roosters at lock or hooker. She is a powerful runner with outstanding ball-handling skills.

THE AIM OF THE GAME

The aim of the game is to put your team in the best field position to be able to score points.

Jaime Chapman

Jaime Chapman plays as a winger for the Brisbane Broncos in the NRL Women's Premiership and the Tweed Heads Seagulls in the QRL Women's Premiership. Chapman has indigenous heritage from the Kamilaroi nation and has represented Australia in the Under-18s Australia Schoolgirl Sevens (2019), Under 18s New South Wales Origin (2019), New South Wales Rugby Sevens (2019), Australian Indigenous OzTag team (2019) and the Indigenous All Stars (2022). She was also named in the 2022 Jillaroos team.

Scoring

By scoring a try, your team earns four points. Converting the try and kicking the ball through the goal posts and over the cross bar will earn your team two points.

Running

Gain ground by running forward, taking on the defenders and passing the ball to a teammate who is able to score. It is important to score from as close to the goal posts as possible to make the conversion kick easier to convert.

Defence

Defence is very important. To defend your end of the field and stop attacking opportunities for the opposition, requires a very committed team.

Emma Tonegato

Tonegato plays for the St George Illawarra Dragons in the NRL Women's Premiership. She comes from a rugby league background and competed at the 2013 Women's Rugby League World Cup. She has the ability to play on the wing or in the centres and was named in the tournament Dream Team for the Amsterdam leg of the Sevens World Series in May 2015.

Isabelle Kelly

Isabelle Maree Kelly plays for the Sydney Roosters in the NRL Women's Premiership. Primarily a centre, she is an Australian and New South Wales representative. Isabelle made her Harvey Norman Jillaroos debut at the 2017 Auckland Nines, before scoring the first Try in the Jillaroos win over New Zealand in the ANZAC Test in her Test Match debut. She was also part of the Jillaroos team that won the 2017 World Cup, scoring two tries in the final. Isabelle is a personal trainer, who represents North Newcastle in the Harvey Norman New South Wales Women's Premiership.

THE RULES

Many of the women's NRL rules are the same as the men's NRL rules, however the women's game lasts for 70 minutes instead of 80.

Kick-off

The 13 members of each team must be situated in their own halves of the pitch at kick-off. The kicker should then send the ball as far downfield as possible into the opposing half. This gives the opposition the most chance of using up all of their six tackles while the ball is near their goal. The side that kicked-off can then gain possession close to their goal.

Play-the-ball

The play-the-ball rule is used to keep play moving after tackles. A player who is tackled and brought down with the ball must immediately pass the ball.

Tackling

A team is allowed to keep possession and play the ball for six tackles, after which the ball is turned over to the opposition unless there is an infringement and the referee calls six again. Tackling is an important part of rugby league. Players must know how to choose the right tackle, execute it with maximum force, keep it legal and make sure the tackle brings a player to the ground.

Field Goal

A field goal can be scored by a drop kick that lands the ball through the goalposts. This earns your team one point. If the player can manage to kick from outside the forty-metre line, the team earns two points.

Scrums

Scrums are formed when there is a knock-on with the ball being dropped by a player and the ball either travels forward or goes out of bounds. Players pack closely together with their heads down to form a scrummage. The ball is placed in the middle of the players and they attempt to gain possession of the ball by moving it out to a teammate on the outer edge of the huddle.

PLAYER POSITIONS

The 13 players in a league side are divided into seven backs and six forwards. With 6 players on the bench.

Numbers

PLAYER
9

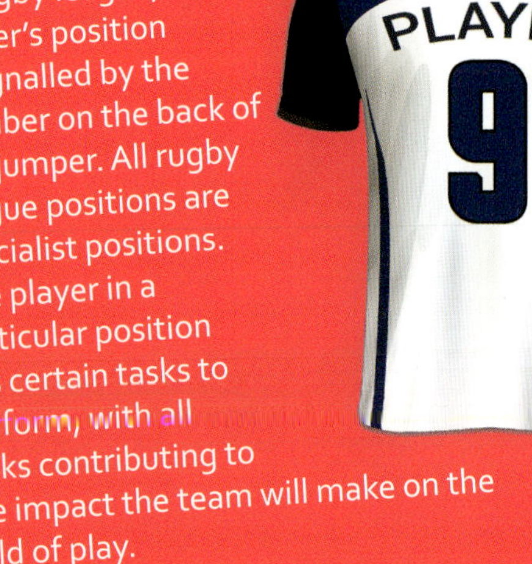

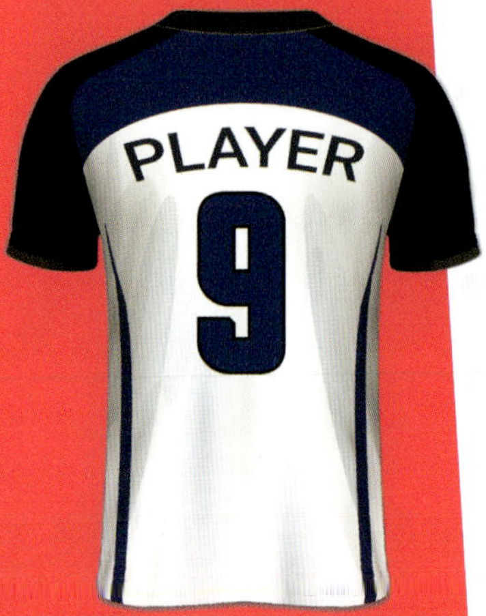

In rugby league, a player's position is signalled by the number on the back of her jumper. All rugby league positions are specialist positions. The player in a particular position has certain tasks to perform, with all tasks contributing to the impact the team will make on the field of play.

Backs

1. Fullback
2. Right winger
3. Right centre
4. Left centre
5. Left winger
6. Five-eighth
7. Halfback or scrumhalf

Forwards

8. Loose-head prop
9. Hooker
10. Tight-head prop
11. Loose-head second row forward
12. Tight-head second row forward
13. Lock forward or loose forward

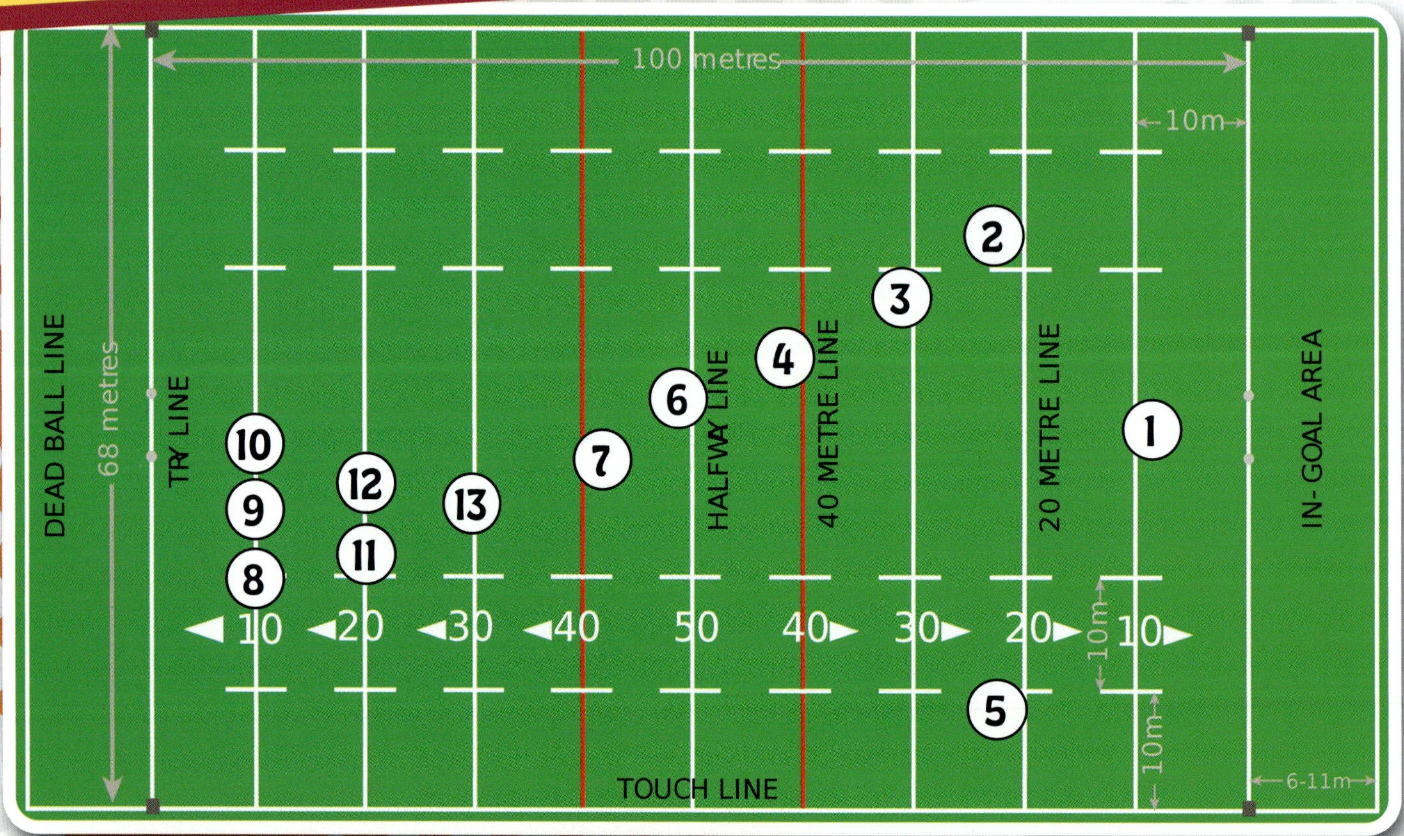

100 metres
10m
68 metres
DEAD BALL LINE
TRY LINE
HALFWAY LINE
40 METRE LINE
20 METRE LINE
IN-GOAL AREA
10 20 30 40 50 40 30 20 10
10m
10m
TOUCH LINE
6-11m
1 2 3 4 5 6 7 8 9 10 11 12 13

Player Roles

1 Fullback

The fullback is the last defender and must be an expert tackler. The fullback also catches high kicks from the opposing team, or gathers the ball up from the ground, initiating counter-attacks. The fullback must be able to withstand particularly heavy tackles, almost from the instant possession is gained.

3 4 Centres

Centres have the job of getting the ball to the wingers, or often of running straight at opposing defenders to draw them away from the wingers. Centres must be speedy, clever and aggressive.

7 Halfback

The halfback (or scrumhalf) is usually one of team's best tacticians. The halfback accepts the ball from the scrum and passes it quickly to the running players to get the attack rolling.

9 Hooker

The hooker is always at the centre of the scrum. They have two tasks; to gain possession of the ball in the scrum and to act as dummy-half in play-the-balls, passing it quickly to attackers.

2 5 Winger

The wingers are the speedsters of the team. They patrol the touchlines, ready to take possession of the ball and head for goal.

6 The Five-Eighth

The five-eighth links the attack at play-the-balls. The five-eighth must know the exact situation of the game at all times and choose the right option for passing.

8 10 Props

The props are powerful players who head the scrum, one each side of the hooker. In attack, the props are expected to withstand defenders' tackles and make well-judged passes.

11 12 Second-Row Forwards

The second-row forwards are among the strongest players in the team. They provide momentum in the scrum. When in attack, they carry the ball as far forwards as possible.

13 Lock Forward

The lock forward is at the rear of the scrum. They keep the scrum balanced and may also take the ball from the scrum to pass it to the halfback.

TRAINING

The athleticism of women playing NRLW has skyrocketed over the last two years, in line with publicity and interest around the women's game. Now much more competitive, players need to train harder, be fitter, stronger and faster.

Day One

Together with the coaching staff, a top player goes over their performance in the last match. Skill errors are highlighted. A program for the week is drawn up, emphasising skill features that require attention. The day's training will be with a specialist coach and divided into aerobic exercise (running, either on a track or on an exercise machine), strengthening exercise in the gym, using weights, tackling drills, evasion drills, kicking drills, and passing drills. The exercise program will work on all the major muscle groups in the body (chest, shoulders, arms, legs, trunk and back). All exercise begins with stretching drills, to protect the ligaments, joints and muscles from injury due to any sudden exertion.

Days Two to Six

The training sections drawn up in the plan on day one are repeated on days two to six, with additional whole-team drills added to the program. It is important that the players share and agree on tactics that they will practise, to make sure that the team has a common approach and mindset when they play games. The senior coach will talk to the players about tactics for the upcoming match and all players will contribute in team meetings when the tactics are discussed. Top players will have any problem areas assessed by a specialist coach.

After the Match

For top players, training for the next game starts almost as soon as a match ends. Players will begin a program of light exercise that helps the body make a soft landing after an exhausting, high effort game. The soft landing program may take the form of swimming laps in a warm pool, followed by stretching exercises in the gym.

Match Day

The match day program will be designed to tone players, without risking exhaustion. Light aerobic exercise followed by relaxation exercises, including yoga, help the players deal with any pre-match anxiety.

Simone Kapari

Head Work

It is just as important to have a sound mental program as it is to have a program for the body. Players can develop doubts and anxieties about their performance that can spoil their game. Rugby league players listen to motivational speakers who can psyche them up for a big match. They attend clinics that teach relaxation and learn to think in a positive way about their skills. Some players practise actualisation, which involves thinking about performing well in the hope that it will translate to improved natural performance during the match.

Young Players

Exercise for young players is never as intense as the programs followed by elite players. Over exertion can harm a young player's development. It is important for young players to develop their bodies without straining them and without risking injury. Talk to your coach or school sport teacher about the best training for you.

Eating to Win

Elite players follow a strict eating program. Professional dietitians and nutritionalists work out special meal plans for each individual player. All of the major food groups are represented in the program including lean protein, essential fatty acids and a wide range of vitamins and minerals from fresh fruits and vegetables. Carbohydrates become more important as match day approaches, since they provide energy for powerful bursts of running and tackling.

NRLW TEAMS 2022

Women's Rugby League is played at many levels in Australia. There are state-based competitions, State of Origin matches, All Stars games and the NRL Premiership competition.

Women's Premiership Captains 2022

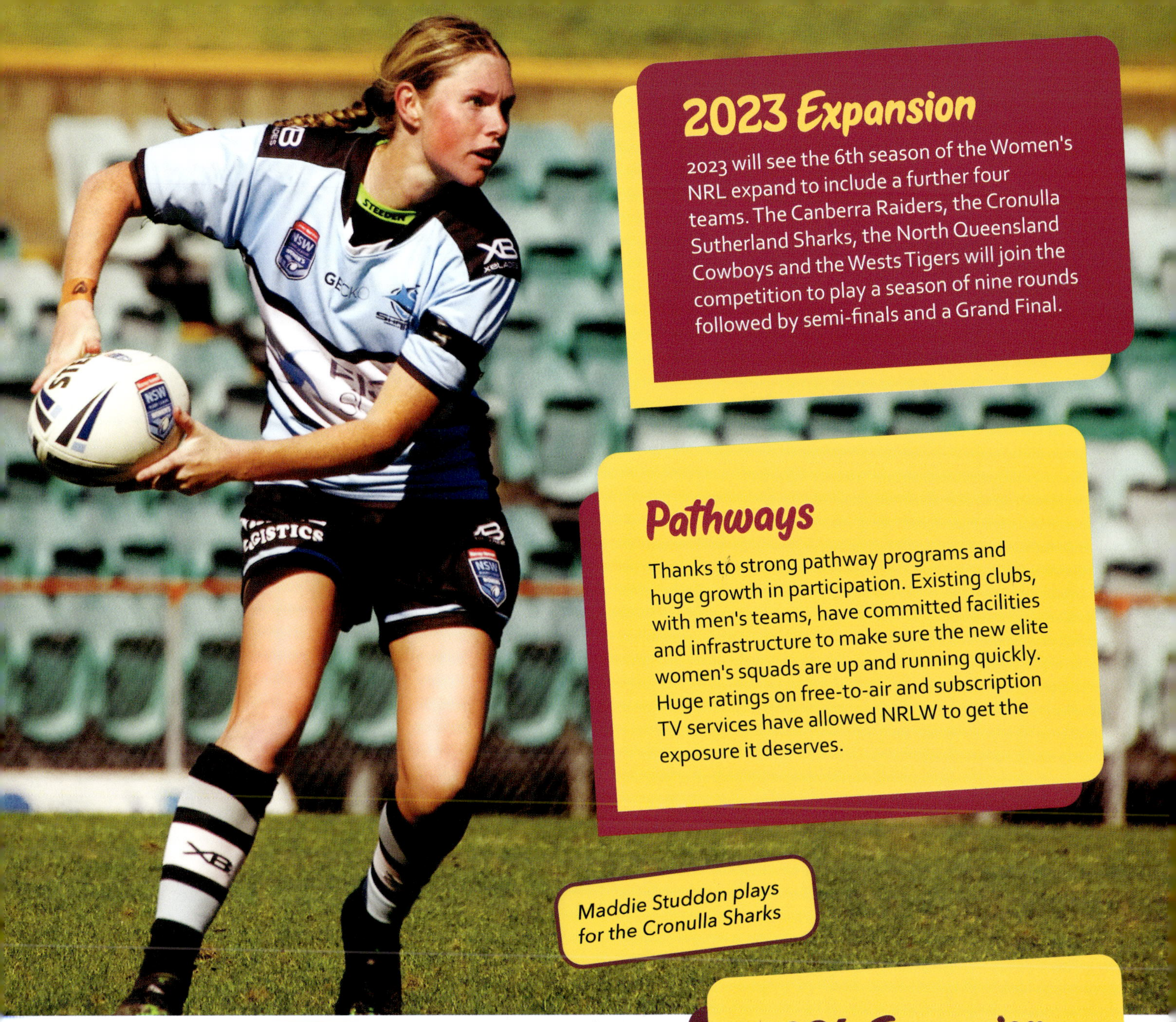

2023 Expansion

2023 will see the 6th season of the Women's NRL expand to include a further four teams. The Canberra Raiders, the Cronulla Sutherland Sharks, the North Queensland Cowboys and the Wests Tigers will join the competition to play a season of nine rounds followed by semi-finals and a Grand Final.

Pathways

Thanks to strong pathway programs and huge growth in participation. Existing clubs, with men's teams, have committed facilities and infrastructure to make sure the new elite women's squads are up and running quickly. Huge ratings on free-to-air and subscription TV services have allowed NRLW to get the exposure it deserves.

Maddie Studdon plays for the Cronulla Sharks

2024 Expansion

More NRLW expansions are expected in 2024, with more clubs submitting proposals to be ready to play. With strong interest from almost every NRL club, it's now only a question of timing. Some clubs are building centres of excellence and some are building their women's teams from the bottom up.

NEW Teams Joining the Women's Premiership in 2023

CANBERRA RAIDERS
WWW.RAIDERS.COM.AU
The Raiders

WESTS TIGERS
WWW.NEWCASTLEKNIGHTS.COM.AU
The Tigers

CRONULLA SHARKS
WWW.SHARKS.COM.AU
The Sharks

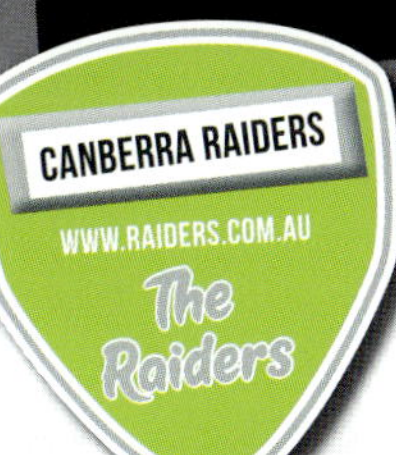

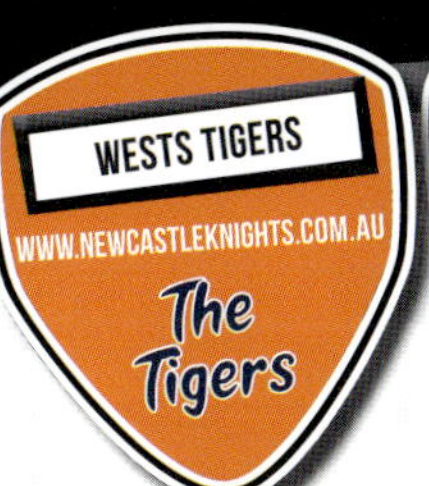

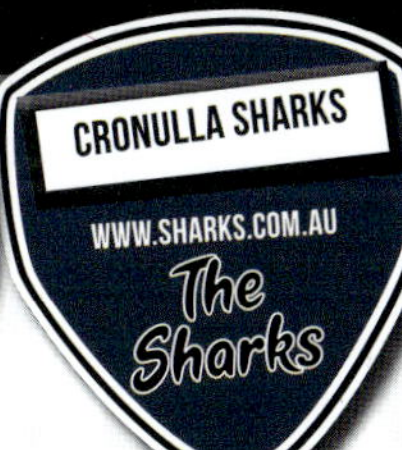

NORTH QUEENSLAND COWBOYS
WWW.COWBOYS.COM.AU
The Cowboys

AWARDS

Each season, the NRLW presents major awards and accolades to its outstanding players.

Dally M Winners

2015 Jenni-Sue Hoepper – Jillaroos
2016 Kezie Apps – Jillaroos
2017 Simaima Taufa – Jillaroos
2018 Brittany Breayley – Brisbane Broncos
2019 Jessica Sergis – St George Illawarra
2020 Ali Brigginshaw – Brisbane Broncos
2021 Emma Tonegato – St George Illawarra and
2021 Millie Boyle – Broncos
2022 Raecene McGregor – Sydney Roosters

In 2021 Emma Tonegato and Millie Boyle shared the NRLW Dally M Medal

NRL Women In League Achievement Award

The NRL Women In League Achievement Award is presented to players who act as advocates for the advancement and opportunity of women in rugby league. The winners are players who raise awareness of women's involvement in rugby league and who play an active role in encouraging more girls and women to play.

Sydney Roosters halfback Raecene McGregor received the 2022 NRLW Dally M Medal

Veronica White Medal

The Veronica White medal recognises female rugby league players in local communities. They are voted on by a panel of experts from across the game. The medal is awarded on Grand Final day each year with nominees announced in the lead-up to the match.

Winners

2019 Honey Hireme-Smiler – Warriors
2020 Georgia Hale – New Zealand Warriors
2021 Karina Brown – Gold Coast Titans
2022 Kennedy Cherrington – Parramatta Eels

Medals and Trophies

Best & Fairest Trophy – for the best and fairest player in the league, voted by the referees.
Leading Try Award – for the player who scores the most tries during the home and away season.
Rookie of the Year – for exceptional players in their first two years of play
Veronica White Medal – for the player who supports their local community
Karyn Murphy Medal – for the best player in the Grand Final, voted by a committee of media members
Karyn Murphy medal – for the player of the match in the NRL Telstra Women's Premiership grand final.
The Dally M Medal – for the 'best and fairest' over the full NRL season

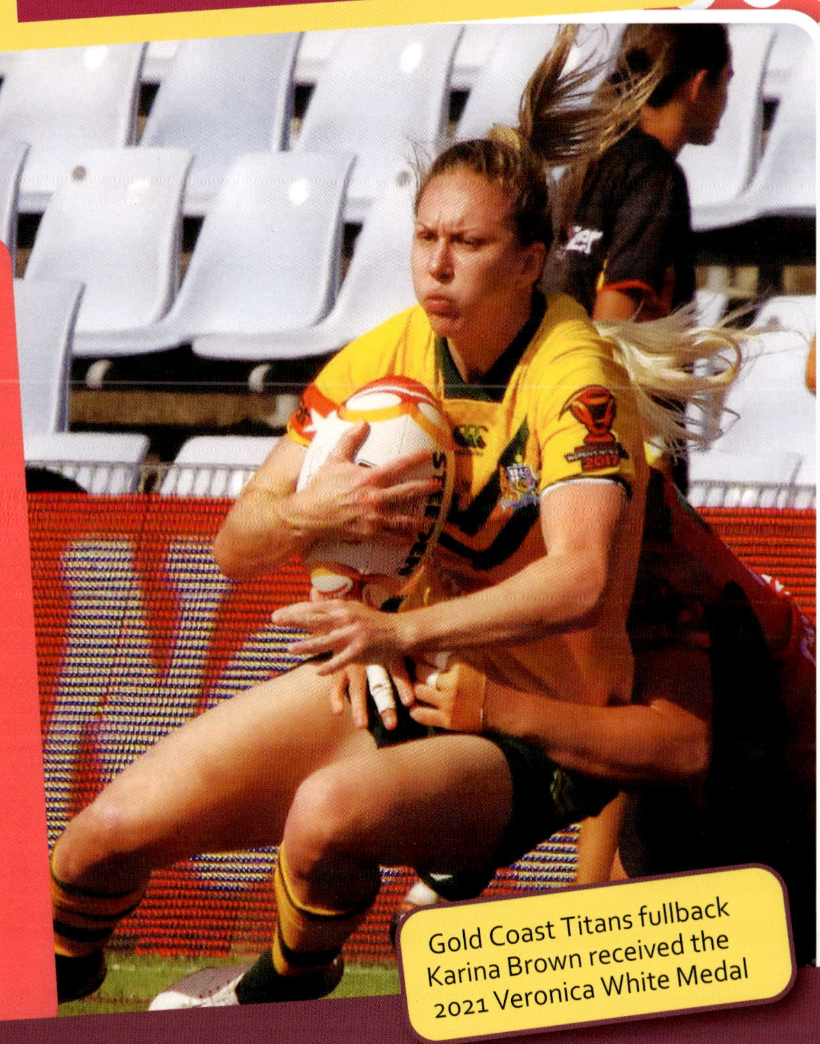
Gold Coast Titans fullback Karina Brown received the 2021 Veronica White Medal

STATE OF ORIGIN

The women's interstate competition between New South Wales and Queensland consists of one game in which teams contest for the newly-made Women's Origin Shield.

Nellie Doherty Cup

The State of Origin game format has been played since 1999 under the name of the Nellie Doherty Cup, but was renamed State of Origin in 2018. The player of the match now receives the Nellie Doherty Medal. Nellie Doherty, together with Molly Cane, were pioneers of the women's game in Australia. In 1921, they were responsible for persuading the New South Wales Rugby League governing body to support and assist in the creation of the first women's competitive league.

Interstate Series

Queensland and New South Wales began an interstate series in 1999, playing for the Nellie Doherty Cup. This ongoing series was called the Women's Interstate Challenge but sometimes spoken of as the Women's State of Origin. Until 2017, teams were chosen based on where the players lived.

NSW
The Blues

Winning Games

2018

2019

2022

QLD
The Maroons

Winning Games

2020

2021

State of Origin

On 6 December 2017, the NRL announced the re-branding of the Women's Interstate Challenge to the Women's State of Origin. Previously, this game was only played as a time-filler, but popular demand saw it upgraded to a stand-alone fixture that was fully televised. Since coming under the State of Origin banner, the Nellie Doherty Cup had to be replaced by a shield, so the player of the match now receives the Nellie Doherty Medal.

New South Wales won the first Women's State of Origin game on 22 June 2018, defeating Queensland 16-10 at North Sydney Oval. Blues' centre Isabelle Kelly, scored two tries in the win and won the inaugural Nellie Doherty Medal.

Game One of the 2023 State of Origin series will be held in neutral territory on Wednesday 31 May at Adelaide Oval

THE WORLD CUP

The World Cup is the pinnacle of the women's game with international teams competing for the chance to be crowned champions of the world.

2000

Since the first Rugby World Cup in women's history in 2000, there have been six tournaments, all hosted in either the United Kingdom, New Zealand or Australia. Only two teams have ever won the competition, Australia in 2013, 2017 and 2022 and New Zealand in 2000, 2004 and 2008. Outside of Australia and New Zealand, only Great Britain (2000) and New Zealand Māori (2005) have managed to reach the final round.

Officials

Pathway Programs across Australia allow potential female officials to develop the technical, physical and personal skills needed for a range of officiating levels including refereeing.

Belinda Sharpe and Kasey Badger

Belinda Sharpe and Kasey Badger are Elite Squad Officials. Sharpe made her official debut as a referee in 2019 after beginning her officiating career in Queensland. She moved to Sydney in 2018 to accept a full-time role as an NRL match official. Badger came through the junior representative development system in Sydney. She is a regular touch judge in NRL.

Kasey Badger is a regular touch judge in NRL

Australia beat the New Zealand Ferns 54-4 at Old Trafford in Manchester, UK

Jillaroos 2022

Tarryn Aiken
Kezie Apps
Shaylee Bent
Samantha Bremner
Ali Brigginshaw
LaurenBrown
Jaime Chapman
Kennedy Cherrington
Shenae Ciesiolka
Yasmin Clydsdale
Keeley Davis
Taliah Fuimaono
Tallisha Harden
Caitlan Johnston
Keilee Joseph
Isabelle Kelly
Olivia Kernick
Shannon Mato
Evania Pelite
Julia Robinson
Jessica Sergis
Simaima Taufa
Emma Tonegato
Holli Wheeler

Coach Brad Donald

Isabelle Kelly

Isabelle Kelly plays as a centre for the Sydney Roosters in the NRL Women's Premiership and the Central Coast Roosters in the NSWRL Women's Premiership. She is also a Jillaroo and a member of the NSW Blues.

INDIGENOUS AND MĀORI ALL STARS

In 2021, the Māori All Stars defeated the Indigenous All Stars women by 24 points to zero. In 2022, the Indigenous All Stars defeated the Māori All Stars by 18 points to eight.

Respect

The Indigenous women's All Stars and the Māori All Stars are two First Nations cultures that come together through rugby league. The Indigenous women's All Stars and the Māori All Stars are two First Nations cultures that come together through rugby league. There is a deep sense of pride on the field and both teams show great respect to one another. Game day is known to showcase a range of cultural performances arts and traditions.

Kirra Dibb

Kirra Dibb is an Australian rugby league footballer who plays for the Newcastle Knights in the NRL Women's Premiership. She made her debut for New South Wales in 2019, starting at five-eighth in their 14–4 win over Queensland. In 2019, Dibb represented three Australian sides – the Prime Minister's XIII in their win over the Fiji Prime Minister's XIII, the Australia 9s team at the 2019 Rugby League World Cup 9s and the Australian Jillaroos in their 28–8 win over New Zealand. She is an Indigenous All Star.

Quincy Dodd

Quincy Dodd is an Australian rugby league footballer who plays for the St George Illawarra Dragons in the NRL Women's Premiership and the Cronulla-Sutherland Sharks in the NSWRL Women's Premiership. She plays as hooker or halfback, is a New South Wales representative and is an Indigenous All Star player.

Indigenous All Stars

Co-captains Caitlan Johnston and Quincy Dodd
1. Tamika Upton **2.** Jaime Chapman **3.** Bobbi Law **4.** Jasmine Peters **5.** Rhiannon Revell-Blair **6.** Kirra Dibb **7.** Tahlulah Tillett **8.** Tommaya Kelly-Sines **9.** Quincy Dodd **10.** Caitlan Johnston **11.** Shaniah Power **12.** Shaylee Bent **13.** Keilee Joseph **14.** Sarah Field **15.** Janelle Williams **16.** Kaitlyn Phillips **17.** Kyra Simon **18.** Taliah Fuimaono.

Māori All Stars

Captain Corban Baxter
1. Botille Vette-Welsh **2.** Jocephy Daniels **3.** Tiana Raftstrand-Smith **4.** Corban Baxter **5.** Autumn-Rain Stephens **6.** Raecene McGregor **7.** Zahara Temara **8.** Shannon Mato **9.** Nita Maynard **10.** Rona Peters **11.** Roxette Murdoch **12.** Olivia Kernick **13.** Kennedy Cherrington **14.** Mya Hill-Moana **15.** Krystal Rota **16.** Rangimarie Edwards Bruce **17.** Lavinia Gould **18.** Katelyn Vahaakolo.

INDEX AND GLOSSARY

ball handling 13
coach 7, 11, 20, 21, 29
diet 21
field goal 15
fouls 31
goal 12, 14-16, 19, 31
Hunter Valley Women's Rugby 4
Jillaroos 6, 10, 24, 29
kicking 12, 15, 20
kick-off 16, 31
New Zealand Ferns 4, 6, 10, 28, 29
passing 12, 14, 19, 20
play-the-ball 16, 19, 31
referee 17, 24, 28
set-piece kick for goal 12
State of Origin 6, 10, 11, 22, 26, 27
tackling 13, 17
training 20, 21
World Cup 6, 10, 28

conversion kick for goal following a try – successful conversion adds a further two points to the points awarded for the try

dummy-half also known as acting halfback, the player who receives the ball in a play-the-ball situation – the role of the dummy half is usually taken by the hooker

evasion movement of the body designed to avoid a tackle

foul an illegal play

infringe commit a foul

kick-off start of play, when the ball is kicked forwards from the centre

knock-on deliberate or accidental movement of the ball forwards using the hands or arms

pass movement of the ball from one player to another

pitch playing field

play-the-ball rule where a tackled player gets to his or her feet and kicks the ball backwards to a teammate

possession control of the ball

professional sportsperson who is paid for playing a sport

scrum formation of players from each team to contest the ball after an infringement and after the ball leaves the field

tackle forcing a player in possession of the ball to the ground

Test match international rugby league match between two evenly matched sides

touchlines side boundaries of the pitch

try score achieved when the ball is legally carried over the goal line and touched on the ground